Your Finances
GOD'S WAY
WORKBOOK

Scott LaPierre

HARVEST HOUSE PUBLISHERS
EUGENE, OREGON

Cover design by Kyler Dougherty

Cover photo © AndreyPopov / Getty Images

Interior design by KUHN Design Group

Published in association with The Blythe Daniel Agency, Inc., P.O. Box 64197, Colorado Springs, CO 80962-4197, www.theblythedanielagency.com.

For bulk, special sales, or ministry purchases, please call 1-800-547-8979.
Email: Customerservice@hhpbooks.com

Your Finances God's Way Workbook
Copyright © 2022 by Scott LaPierre
Published by Harvest House Publishers
Eugene, Oregon 97408
www.harvesthousepublishers.com

ISBN 978-0-7369-8402-7 (pbk)
ISBN 978-0-7369-8403-4 (eBook)

Printed in the United States of America

22 23 24 25 26 27 28 29 30 / BP / 10 9 8 7 6 5 4 3 2 1

Contents

Welcome

Finances are one of our most important stewardships. If for no other reason than that, we should want to manage them well. So, let me commend you—you went beyond simply reading *Your Finances God's Way* to also purchasing this accompanying workbook. You are investing time and energy (spiritual, mental, and emotional) to learn how to handle money in ways that please God and bring Him glory.

KEEPING GOD'S WORD IN YOUR HEART

As a pastor, I've spent numerous hours doing counseling. The time with people has given me familiarity with the most common problems people face. I have seen them struggle and then find the solutions in God's Word, which provides us with wisdom for every area of life, including finances. When I ask you to trust God's Word, I do so because I have seen it work in my life as well as the lives of people I've counseled.

This workbook is designed to encourage practical application and bring real change (because that's what applying scriptural truth does—it brings about change). For this to happen, we must keep God's Word in our heart, as it repeatedly reminds us:

- "These words that I command you today *shall be on your heart*" (Deuteronomy 6:6).

- "The *law of his God is in his heart*; his steps do not slip" (Psalm 37:31).

- "I delight to do your will, O my God; *your law is within my heart*" (Psalm 40:8).

- "I have *stored up your word in my heart*, that I might not sin against you" (Psalm 119:11).

- "Receive instruction from his mouth, and *lay up his words in your heart*" (Job 22:22).

While *Your Finances God's Way* is not the Word of God, it is a guide filled with the Word of God. I have written this workbook to help you apply the teaching from the book and keep God's Word in your heart. As Jesus said, "The good soil, they are those who, hearing the word, *hold it fast in an honest and good heart*" (Luke 8:15).

BEING A DOER VERSUS ONLY A READER

From years of weightlifting, I've had lower back issues. I'll go to the physical therapist and learn the stretches and exercises I'm supposed to do at home, but I rarely do them. My wonderful wife, Katie, repeatedly says, "Why do you go to those appointments if you're not going to do what you're told?" I don't have a good answer. My actions indicate that I think simply going to the appointments helps me, but I'm deceiving myself.

We make the same mistake when we read scriptural truth but fail to apply it to our lives. James 1:22 says, "Be doers of the word, and not hearers only, *deceiving yourselves*." This verse reveals a common mistake I make with the physical therapist and many of us make with God's Word: We learn it without applying it to our lives.

We do this with our finances when we believe we have done enough simply by learning what the Bible teaches about money, reading Christian finance books, and attending Christian conferences or Bible studies on money. But as believers, our responsibility goes much further than simply obtaining information. We must also apply it, or none of the knowledge we gain will be of any benefit. We do not learn God's Word simply for the sake of acquiring knowledge. We learn it so that we can apply it and better serve the Lord. Jesus said, "My mother and My brothers are those who hear the word of God *and do it*… If you know these things, blessed are you *if you do them*" (Luke 8:21; John 13:17 NKJV). He also taught an entire parable making this point:

> Everyone then who hears these words of mine *and does them* will be like a wise man who built his house on the rock. And the rain fell, and the floods came, and the winds blew and beat on that house,

but it did not fall, because it had been founded on the rock. And everyone who hears these words of mine *and does not do them* will be like a foolish man who built his house on the sand. And the rain fell, and the floods came, and the winds blew and beat against that house, and it fell, and great was the fall of it (Matthew 7:24-27).

I would like to begin our journey through the *Your Finances God's Way Workbook* with a look at this parable for two reasons:

1. Jesus brought the Sermon on the Mount to a close with this teaching. He wanted to make sure His listeners put into practice what they heard. My prayer is that this workbook will help you put into practice what you have read in the accompanying book.

2. This teaching makes clear that there is only one true foundation for any area of our lives, including our finances: Jesus Christ.

Be encouraged that you are off to a great start being not just a hearer (or reader), but a doer (or obey-er) by using this workbook.

FINANCIAL STORMS WILL COME

Why is it so important to have a strong foundation? Jesus revealed the need this way: "The rain fell, and the floods came, and the winds blew" (Matthew 7:25). You have probably seen on the news—or perhaps personally experienced—what can happen to a house under the onslaught of a powerful storm, hurricane, tornado, or tsunami. Jesus was not teaching that the weather will be unpleasant or chilly and we might need an umbrella or coat to protect ourselves. Rather, He was speaking of the inevitable trials that we all experience (see John 16:33; Acts 14:22; 1 Thessalonians 3:3; James 1:2; 1 Peter 4:12).

The words "beat on that house" in Matthew 7:25 are analogous to the struggles that wear on us. Financially speaking, this could be a job loss, bills that pile up, stock market crash, or car accident. Not only are many of these storms financial, statistics show financial storms are the most common we face. Since the *American Psychological Association* began their survey in 2007, "Stress in America: Paying with Our Health," each year they found that money is people's most common cause of stress.[1] A survey conducted by Northwestern Mutual had similar findings: Money is the primary source of stress for 44 percent of people, followed by 25 percent who said personal relationships, and 18 percent who cited work.[2] In the same way that physical storms have the potential to knock down a house, financial storms have the potential to make us feel as though we are going to collapse. How many people have said, "I can't pay this anymore…I don't know how we are going to make ends meet…I will lose my mind if we get one more bill"?

Let's note what Jesus was *not* teaching in this parable: Obeying Him keeps us from experiencing storms. Sometimes we think that if we are "good Christians," then God will prevent trials, including financial ones, from coming our way. This is prosperity theology, also known as health-and-wealth doctrine, and it is false. Note that Jesus said the storms were beating on a house that *was* built on the strong foundation of His teaching.

If obeying Jesus's teaching does not enable us to avoid the financial storms of life, then what is the benefit of obedience? Jesus promised that obedience enables us to survive the storms: "The rain fell, and the floods came, and the winds blew and beat on that house, but *it did not fall, because it had been founded on the rock*" (Matthew 7:25). Obeying Jesus's teachings will not help us *avoid* financial storms, but it will help us *survive* them.

Perhaps you have witnessed people experiencing a financial difficulty and thought, *How can they handle that? I don't know what I would do if that were me!* The great encouragement is that if you are obeying Jesus's teachings, you can be assured that you, too, will be able to withstand.

THE IMPORTANCE OF OBEDIENCE

If we are not building on Christ—which is to say we are not obeying the commands in Scripture—then we should not have much confidence that we will survive the financial storms of life. Jesus made this clear when He said, "The rain fell, the floods came, and the winds blew and beat against that house, and *it fell*, and *great was the fall of it*" (Matthew 7:27). Jesus's words are strong, but was He being harsh? Just the opposite! He was being loving. He wanted to convince us to build our lives on the Word of God.

The Sermon on the Mount is filled with incredible teaching for every believer, but those who familiarize themselves with its teachings without obeying are no better off than those with no familiarity with the teaching. *Your Finances God's Way* is a book filled with the Bible's counsel on money, but if you do not obey what Scripture says, you will be no better off than those who never read the book in the first place. Christ is the strong foundation we need in our lives so that we can manage our finances well, but that requires us to *do*, and not merely *read*.

Response Determines Outcome

The accounts of the wise and the foolish builders are almost identical:

- They both seem to be talented builders.

- There was nothing to indicate any difference in their houses; they both achieved the goal of building strong, sturdy houses.

- They faced the same storms; verses 25 and 27 say that "the rain fell, and the floods came, and the winds blew and beat against that house."

This is why the two widely differing results are so shocking: "it did not fall" versus "it fell. And great was its fall." The builders had nearly identical circumstances, but completely different outcomes. The only noteworthy difference was the foundation under each house.

Similarly, it is not the size of our paychecks or the amounts in our checking, savings, and retirement accounts that is of greatest importance. Instead, it is the foundation we are building on.

Wisdom and Foolishness Revealed

In *Your Finances God's Way* I wrote:

> More wisdom is required with finances than most parts of the Christian life…Solomon was the richest man ever to live. First Kings 10:21 says, "All King Solomon's drinking vessels were gold…Not one was silver, for this was accounted as nothing in the days of Solomon." He had such an obsession with money that he accumulated enough gold to cause silver to become worthless. Yet he still recognized wisdom's greater value: "How much better to get wisdom than gold!" (Proverbs 16:16)…

> This book is primarily about money, but it's important to keep wisdom's greater value in mind because "a foolish man devours [precious treasure]" (Proverbs 21:20 NIV). This verse is often loosely quoted as, "A fool and his money are soon parted." Unwise people waste money and spend it so carelessly that they soon find themselves penniless. To put it simply: Those who lack wisdom will lack money no matter how much they make. No amount of money is enough for foolish people who don't know how to manage it well because they will soon be separated from it…

The wisdom we need is found in God's Word. Second Timothy 3:17 says Scripture allows us to "be complete, thoroughly equipped for every good work," and this includes the managing our finances. The following chapters will provide an abundance of guidance from Bible verses because if we are going to do things God's way, we need to know (and obey) what God's Word says! (pages 17-18).

Because wisdom is so important, let's ensure we understand it. We typically associate wisdom with knowledge: People are wise when they have some measure of knowledge. Conversely, we associate foolishness with a lack of knowledge. But knowledge doesn't make people wise any more than a lack of knowledge makes people foolish. The lack of knowledge simply means people are ignorant. Thus, when the apostle Paul wrote to people who were ignorant, he gave them knowledge versus condemning them.[3]

If foolishness isn't the lack of knowledge, then what is it? A good definition of foolish is "failing to apply knowledge." A good definition of wise is "applying knowledge." Consider the builders in the parable. They both heard the same teachings of Jesus, which means they had the same knowledge. The wise builder was wise because he applied what he heard, and the foolish builder was foolish because he did not.

I would like to again commend you because in purchasing this workbook, you've taken a big step toward applying the knowledge you've learned (or will learn) in *Your Finances God's Way*. But keep in mind your wisdom or foolishness is not shown by how much knowledge you gain from the book. Rather, it is shown by whether you apply that knowledge. Here's the simple yet crucial truth: Managing our finances God's way means having Christ's teaching as the foundation.

THE BENEFIT OF WRITING ON LEARNING

What better way to apply what you have read than to answer the questions in the following chapters? I am confident your investment will pay great dividends, for two reasons. First, the instruction in *Your Finances God's Way* is drawn from the Bible. Haggai 2:8 says, "The silver is mine, and the gold is mine, declares the Lord of hosts." As the owner of all wealth, God knows what we must do to manage money well.

The second reason I'm confident your investment in the workbook will pay dividends is less spiritual and more practical. Before becoming a pastor, I was an elementary schoolteacher. That's when I learned how people learn. When I started preaching—telling people to open their Bibles versus telling students to open their math books—it was another form (albeit infinitely more important) of teaching. Whether I'm delivering a sermon, speaking at a conference, or guest preaching, I do my best to provide those in attendance with handouts that have lessons and blanks to fill in.

Why do I do this? Most of us retain only a small amount of what we read. This is unfortunate because of the importance of going beyond hearing or reading to applying and obeying. As you probably know, people retain more information when they take notes versus only listen.[4] But did you know their retention is even better when the notes are handwritten versus typed?[5]

Maybe it's been a while since you've written much by hand. We've moved away from letters to emails and many of us rely on our computers all day. But you can be encouraged in knowing the answers in this workbook will have a much better chance of staying with you because you wrote them down. Another added benefit is you will have a record you can refer to in the future. It is always exciting and humbling to see how God changes us along our journey.

USING THIS WORKBOOK

I know you are eager to begin, and here are three guidelines that will enable you to receive the most benefit from the *Your Finances God's Way Workbook*:

1. There are questions for each section of the book. Read the corresponding section in the book before you look at the workbook questions.

2. Instead of reading an entire chapter of the book and then answering the questions, it is best to read one section at a time, and then answer the corresponding questions.

3. Do not rush the reading or hurry to answer the questions. Take your time and pray. Reflecting and meditating on what you are reading and writing will give you the most benefit and allow God to be part of the process.

Let's begin this journey together with the Bible as our guide and the Holy Spirit as our Helper. We are on our way to experiencing the blessings of managing our finances God's way.

I have been praying for you, will continue to, and if you have any specific requests for me, I invite you to please let me know. I would love to hear from you about how God is helping you manage your finances.

Your brother in Christ,
Scott LaPierre
www.scottlapierre.org/contact

One of Our Most Important Stewardships

All of us have experienced financial difficulties in the past, and we will experience more in the future. Many of these difficulties can negatively affect almost every area of our lives. My hope is that by applying the wisdom you will learn in the following chapters, then at best these problems can be avoided, and at worst they can be mitigated.

Statistically speaking, we are some of the wealthiest people who have ever lived. Many of us don't need to become wealthier. Instead, we need to learn to stretch our wealth further and in ways that please and glorify the Lord. When we first take the time to focus on our hearts, our decisions and actions will come in line with God's will, because when you shape the heart, you will shape your behavior.

Live off less money than you make, and you'll be prepared if you ever really must live off less money than you make!

Explain the biggest financial crisis you have faced.

What did you learn from the situation? In hindsight, is there anything you would do differently? If so, what?

In what way(s) did you see God provide?

Have you already thought of any ways you can live off less money than you make? If so, what are they?

SOME CREDIBILITY AND ENCOURAGEMENT

God knows what you should and shouldn't do with your finances, and He has provided you with the needed instructions in His Word.

Why can we be confident that God knows best what we should do with our finances?

Why do you think finances can be one of the most common problem areas in a marriage?

Discuss three blessings you have seen from obeying God's Word.

Discuss three negative consequences you have seen from disobeying God's Word.

We will talk about paying off debt in more detail in future chapters, but what can you start telling yourself even now in preparation?

What does it mean that God's Word deals with our hearts versus our bank accounts?

How can managing your finances better provide you with greater freedom?

What application does Jesus's miracle with the fish and loaves and Elisha's miracle with the widow's oil have for our finances?

Suggest three ways you can honor God with your finances.

Do you think about finances too little or too much?

THE PROBLEM WITH MONEY PROBLEMS

*Aside from health issues and rebellious children,
few things cause as much anxiety as finances.*

In what ways do financial problems cause you anxiety?

In what ways have financial problems negatively affected your marriage and family?

What relationships and areas of your life can be improved by managing your finances better?

"ARE YOU GOING TO HELP ME BECOME RICH?"

*Coveting and the love of money can be destructive, so
I wouldn't want to steer you in that direction.*

Financially speaking, what are three behaviors you need to put off?

Financially speaking, what are three behaviors you need to put on?

HOW WEALTHY ARE WE?

---

*If you live in America, measured by the living standards of the
rest of the world, and especially those throughout history,
you live in the wealthiest nation that has ever existed.*

Why is it important to keep in mind that we are some of the wealthiest people
who have ever lived?

FINANCES REQUIRE WISDOM

---

*More wisdom is required with finances than
most parts of the Christian life.*

Why is wisdom so important when it comes to managing our finances?

Why are foolish people quickly parted from their money?

THE APPROACH TAKEN IN THE FOLLOWING CHAPTERS

What good is there in learning what to do without a heart to obey?

Why don't the early chapters of *Your Finances God's Way* contain much application?

What does it mean to deal with the spiritual versus the physical?

OUR RELATIONSHIP WITH MONEY REFLECTS OUR RELATIONSHIP WITH CHRIST

We should handle our finances well not because we want to be rich, but because we want to please our Lord and Savior.

Why do you think Jesus talked so much about money?

Why do our financial decisions say so much about our faith?

We handle our finances the way we do because of our relationship with Christ. Keep in mind that we do what we do with our money—from spending and saving to giving—as an outflow of our relationship with our Savior.

As we consider everything Jesus has done for us, how can we not be motivated to handle money in ways that most please Him? Before finishing this chapter, spend some time praying. Thank God for all He has done for you and ask Him to give you the grace to apply what you learn in the following chapters.

CHAPTER 1

Stewardship and Faithfulness

All the wealth throughout human history has belonged to God. This truth should cause us to view every cent differently. Instead of seeing ourselves as owners of money, we see ourselves as humble stewards.

Few places, if any, in all of Scripture can challenge us to be good stewards like the parable of the talents. It wouldn't be too much to say that the main point of this teaching from our Lord is to encourage us to use, for His glory, what He has given us.

Your money isn't your money! It's God's money.

How does our view of finances change when we understand all money belongs to God?

ENCOURAGED BY THE PARABLE OF THE TALENTS

If you've ever put someone in charge of something that belongs to you, you know the one thing you value more than anything else is faithfulness.

What does it mean to be a steward?

Why is it so important for stewards to be faithful?

In the parable, what do each of the following represent?

- The man:

- The far country:

- The servants:

- The talents:

Considering what a talent represents, what do you think are the five most important talents in your life?

GOD JUDGES CHRISTIANS' STEWARDSHIPS VERSUS THEIR SINS

If you're in Christ, you will never stand before the Great White Throne, which is the terrifying judgment at which unbelievers will learn they will pay for their sins.

Why must unbelievers stand before the Great White Throne?

What will it be like for believers when we stand before the Judgment Seat of Christ?

Considering we will give an account to Christ, are there any changes you want to make in your life? If so, what are they?

Do you recognize any competing desires that can distract you from Christ? If so, what can you do to prevent them from causing you to be unfaithful?

First, God Gives What We Should Have or What We Can Handle

God does not overestimate or underestimate our abilities.

How do the words "according to his abilities" reveal God is equitable even though people receive different numbers of talents?

When we are unfaithful, does that mean God made a mistake in the number of talents He gave us? Explain your answer.

Second, God Judges Our Proportion Versus Our Portion

The Lord expects more from those who have been given more...[and] less from those who have been given less.

Why did the second servant receive the same reward as the first, even though he produced less than half as much?

Third, God Does Not Compare Us with Others

Why should we not compare ourselves with others?

The First Danger of Comparing: Discouragement

How can comparing yourself with others be discouraging?

The Second Danger of Comparing: Pride

The standard is faithfulness to what God expects of us, not what others are doing.

How can comparing yourself with others lead to pride?

THE SAME REWARD FOR GOING TO BATTLE AND GUARDING THE SUPPLIES

Just as David rewarded the 600 men equally...the master rewarded the two servants equally because they were equally faithful.

Discuss a time the wisdom of one of your decisions was justified, or shown right, by what was produced.

Why weren't the 200 men able to go further, and why did David go out to greet them?

Why did David reward all 600 men equally, and what application does this have for our finances?

ARE YOU THE 400, 200, FIRST SERVANT, OR SECOND SERVANT?

In the Day of Judgment the only question that will matter is, "Have we been faithful with the ability God's given us?"

Financially speaking, do you think you're more like the 200 men or the 400 men? In other words, do you think God expects you to give more or less than others?

Do you think you're being faithful with what God has entrusted to you? If yes, why? If no, what changes can you begin making even at this time to be more faithful?

Regarding your roles and responsibilities, how can you please God?

What two or three concrete actions can you take to be "faithful" tomorrow?

Hopefully, the parable of the talents has left you motivated to be a good steward. I know that's the case for me every time I read it. Please conclude this chapter being encouraged by three truths:

1. God isn't giving us more than we can faithfully steward.

2. God is judging our proportion versus our portion.

3. We don't need to compare ourselves with others; we only need to strive to be faithful with what we have been given.

Let's keep these blessings in mind as we move into the following chapters and learn how to manage our finances God's way.

CHAPTER 2

God's Kindness and Severity

———————

We should approach God's Word committed to believing what it teaches whether we disagree, it seems too good to be true, or it doesn't make sense. Most people who have studied the Bible have experienced all three of these scenarios. In such times, we must choose to embrace what we are reading.

One such situation might very well occur when we see what God has in store for believers and unbelievers. The blessings for believers almost seem too good to be true, while the punishment awaiting unbelievers might seem disagreeable to us.

———————

When we describe God with some of His attributes but
leave out others, we create a false god, or idol.

———————

How could I (and others) believe in God but not yet be a Christian?

Why is it so important to consider all of God's attributes and not just those that are most attractive to us?

THE MASTER'S KINDNESS TO THE FAITHFUL SERVANTS

We will receive more from [God] than we have done for Him.

Why can we be encouraged even if we have been faithful over only a few small things? Note: this is assuming God has called us to be faithful over only a few small things.

What do the words "I will set you over much" reveal about the master's character?

Consider your current thoughts about God. Do you view Him as a gracious, loving heavenly Father who wants to lavish His children with good gifts (James 1:17)? Or do you view Him as a miserly old Scrooge? Explain your answer.

Bringing God Joy

If ever we start to feel as though we're just one of many Christians and, therefore, we're insignificant to the Lord, we should turn to Luke 15 and read these parables.

What seems to bring God the most joy, and why do you think this is the case?

Experiencing God's Joy

God's joy will be part of our reward.

Read about each of the five crowns and then explain which one is your favorite, and why.

THE MASTER'S SEVERITY TO THE UNFAITHFUL SERVANT

If he [the third servant] knew the master was "a hard man," he should've taken his stewardship even more seriously.

What are some of the common criticisms you've heard of God's severity?

What can you tell yourself if you ever start to struggle with God's severity?

Why was the master so angry with the third servant?

What excuses did the third servant give, and why did they fail?

How can we use the money God has given us for His glory?

People Can Be Wicked Because of What They Don't Do

---

*None of us do all the good God wants us to do, but if
our lives are characterized by failing to do the good
God wants, then we can be wicked in His eyes.*

Why was the third servant wicked even though he might not look to us as though he had done anything wicked?

Provide an example of a sin of commission, and a sin of omission.

The Master Expects Something

---

*If anyone looked as though he could have gotten away
without producing anything, it is [the third servant],
yet God still expected something from him.*

Why is it both encouraging and sobering that the master expected interest?

Why was the master upset, and why wasn't he upset?

Are We Saved by Works?

---

*We aren't saved by works, but works are one
of the evidences of being saved.*

What happened to the third servant, and why?

Explain the relationship between faith and works.

What is the main difference between a living faith and a dead faith?

What do works reveal? What about the absence of works?

Faithful Versus Unfaithful Servants

---

*If they had not gone out...they would've looked like Christians until
they stood before the Lord and heard the words of Matthew 25:30.*

What allows people to look like Christians when they are not, and what finally
reveals their insincerity?

Use or Possibly Lose What God's Given You

The unfaithful servant...didn't use what God
gave him, and it was taken from him.

Are there any talents in your life that could possibly be taken away because you are not using them?

BELIEVERS AND UNBELIEVERS EXPERIENCE THE EXTREMES OF GOD'S KINDNESS AND SEVERITY

As Christians, we inherit eternal life. This alone is tremendous,
but we also receive other immeasurable blessings.

Describe the extreme believer's experience.

Describe the extreme unbeliever's experience.

Should we strive to be faithful because of what we receive in return? Not ultimately. We should strive to be faithful because of what God has done for us through His Son, Jesus Christ. But with that said, in Scripture, God does discuss rewards for our faithfulness, which lets us know He wants us not just aware of them but looking forward to them.

Let's keep this in mind as we move into the following chapters. What greater incentives can we have for managing our finances God's way than hearing the wonderful words of our Lord on that day? "Well done, good and faithful servant. You have been faithful over a little; I will set you over much. Enter into the joy of your master" (Matthew 25:21). Oh, that each of us would live in anticipation of hearing these words!

CHAPTER 3

Money Is the Foundation of Faithfulness

Would you believe that Christians can learn from the example of non-Christians? We can. There are some things that unbelievers take more seriously than believers. So yes, we can look at the actions of non-Christians and be challenged by them.

Do you agree with the following statement: "If people can't be faithful with money, they can't be faithful with much else"? I hope so, because it's one of the main points Jesus makes in His most controversial parable, which we will look at in detail (and I believe be blessed by) in this chapter.

Stewards were trusted servants because they had full authority over their master's possessions and could conduct business transactions in the master's name.

Read Luke 16:1-13, and then answer the following two questions:

In your own words, why is this parable potentially confusing?

Though the steward is dishonest, do you see anything that can be commended?

WAS JESUS APPLAUDING DISHONESTY OR DOING SOMETHING ELSE?

Jesus was contrasting two groups—unbelievers and believers. He was saying unbelievers do some things better than believers.

What was Jesus *not* commending in this parable?

What was Jesus doing with this parable?

Who was Jesus rebuking, and why?

The Steward Took Seriously that He Would Give an Account

Some unbelievers take more seriously that they'll stand before an earthly, human master—whether a boss or employer—and give an account, than believers take seriously that they'll stand before their Master, the God of heaven and earth, and give an account.

What changes should you make to show that you take seriously that you will give an account?

Why should we be motivated to be faithful to Christ?

The Steward Prepared for the Future

Unbelievers are shrewder when they deal with the affairs of this life than believers are when they deal with the affairs of the next life.

In what way does the unjust steward model how we should prepare for the future?

How should our view of our finances change in light of eternity?

Are you preparing as well (or better) for your eternity as you are for the remaining years of your earthly life? Explain your answer.

The Steward Knew He Had a Narrow Window of Time to Use His Master's Resources

Are we using to the fullest what the Master has entrusted to us for His glory and honor?

What can we learn from the way the steward took advantage of his master's resources?

What do you have at your disposal that you can use during the narrow window of time you have been given?

The Steward Worked Hard

What if Christians worked as hard for God's kingdom as unbelievers work for their earthly kingdom?

Do you work as hard for God's kingdom as you work in your earthly job? Explain your answer.

Have you committed more early mornings and late evenings to your job or to your relationship with Christ? Explain your answer.

The Steward Used Money to Make Friends

Every believer is a brother or sister in Christ, but Jesus says people who come to salvation because of our giving are friends we have made for ourselves "by means of unrighteous wealth."

Even if we give in many other ways, if we are not giving financially, why are we still disobeying God?

Are you making friends for yourself for eternity? Explain your answer.

Principle One: If We Can't Be Faithful with Money, We Can't Be Faithful with Much Else

----

> *If we can't be faithful with earthly wealth, we can't get rid of our training wheels and be entrusted with heavenly wealth.*

How does our faithful stewardship of earthly treasure speak to our stewardship of eternal treasures?

Why are spiritual riches so much more important than earthly riches?

Principle Two: Serving God or Money

> *Jesus isn't commanding us not to "serve God and money."...* *He's telling us we can't serve Him and money.*

Provide three examples of imperatives from Scripture.

Provide three examples of indicatives from Scripture.

Why can't we serve God and money?

WE MUST CHOOSE

To serve money is to be unfaithful to God, and to be faithful to God means refusing to serve money.

Describe the choice we face.

After honestly examining yourself, if you find that you love money more than you love God, describe how you will repent.

Do you feel challenged by the examples of some unbelievers in your life? They often

- take seriously that they will give an account
- prepare for the future
- know they're dealing with a limited amount of time
- use the money they have to make friends

Are we doing the same? If unbelievers are that serious about their earthly lives, how much more seriously should we take our eternal lives? If you are feeling challenged—as I know I am—keep in mind that God is with you, helping you to make any necessary changes in your life as you seek to live for Him. Before you move on to the next chapter, pray that God gives you the necessary patience, strength, and wisdom.

CHAPTER 4

The Dangers of Loving Money

———

We frequently think in terms of good and bad, which is really to say we ask, "Is this moral or immoral?" But we should also ask, "Is this amoral?" Learning what is moral, immoral, and amoral is important so we can make decisions that please God. Money is a particularly important topic in this discussion because there is so much confusion about it. For example, people think money is immoral when it is amoral, and they think the way they spend money (and even feel about it) is amoral when it is moral or immoral.

"Money is the root of all evil!" We've all heard this quote before, haven't we? Is it true? No. But with a few small adjustments, we can learn the important truths of 1 Timothy 6:10: "The *love of money* is a root of all kinds of evils." Let's jump into this workbook chapter to apply what we've learned about morality and the dangers of loving money.

———

When people rigorously neglect the amoral and follow legalistic, man-made commands, there's "an appearance of wisdom," but there's "no value against [indulging] the flesh," which is to say there's no spiritual benefit.

———

Read Luke 9:23 and then answer the following two questions:

What did Jesus mean when He said these words?

What did Jesus *not* mean when He said these words?

What does it look like for people to rigorously neglect the amoral and follow legalistic, man-made commands? Provide three examples.

MISTAKE 1: THINKING SOMETHING IS AMORAL WHEN IT IS MORAL OR IMMORAL

————————

Most people know their speech is moral, but they might not know that the amount they speak (and listen) is also moral (versus amoral).

————————

What is something immoral that people might think is amoral? Explain what causes this confusion.

MISTAKE 2: THINKING SOMETHING IS IMMORAL WHEN IT IS AMORAL

————————

Food is amoral, but our relationship to it is moral.

————————

What is something amoral that people might think is immoral? Explain what causes this confusion.

THE AMORAL NATURE OF MONEY

Being rich or poor is not moral or immoral,
righteous or sinful, because money itself is amoral.

What does it mean that money is amoral?

How do we know that money is amoral?

Why do some people think money is immoral?

How We Spend Money Is Moral

We can tell what our priorities are by
looking at our checkbook and calendar.

Why is every one of our purchases moral or immoral?

What are three ways we can spend money morally?

What are three ways we can spend money immorally?

Why does our treatment of money say so much about our character?

How We Feel About Money Is Moral

———————

*[When] people [are] fixated on riches it
controls their lives, and this is the danger.*

———————

Why is our relationship with money moral?

Why do so many verses warn us against loving money?

THE LOVE OF MONEY, VERSUS MONEY, IS THE PROBLEM

———————

*It's not right to think money is immoral or responsible for
evil because that puts the blame in the wrong place.*

———————

What's wrong with thinking money is the root of all evil?

Do an honest assessment: How do you feel about money?

TRAPPED BY THE LOVE OF MONEY

How does the love of money snare people?

Loving Money Leads to Sin

The desire to be rich leads to temptation because this leads people to be willing to do almost anything to reach their goal.

Why is loving money so dangerous?

What can you do to develop contentment so that you avoid loving money?

Can you think of other individuals in Scripture whose love of money led to sin?

Loving Money Hurts Others

Can you think of some other ways loving money hurts others?

Loving Money Ruins and Destroys

---

*Loving money is also a trap, because it will "plunge
people into ruin and destruction" (1 Timothy 6:9).*

Why is loving money so destructive?

What are the consequences in this life of loving money?

What are the consequences in the next life for loving money?

Loving Money Requires Repentance

---

*Nobody wants to think they would walk away from the
Lord...The rich young ruler did because he loved money.*

How did Jesus try to get the rich young ruler to recognize his sinfulness and
need for a Savior?

Why do you think the rich young ruler thought he had kept all the commandments?

What is the relationship between covetousness and idolatry?

How did the love of money cause the rich young ruler to walk away from the Lord?

In Scripture, what does it mean if a passage is descriptive versus prescriptive?

We can easily pass judgment on the rich young ruler, but we are also sinful and must repent. What sin do you struggle with that must be repented of most often, and what steps can you take to try to develop victory over it?

CHOKING CHRIST OUT OF OUR LIVES

We can have only so many things occupying space in our hearts.

Why do you think the rich young ruler valued earthly riches more than heavenly riches?

Why do you think it is so difficult for rich people to enter heaven?

Why must we be so careful about what we allow to take up room in our hearts?

As you contemplate what you read in this chapter about money, pray God would reveal any areas of your life that need to change. In particular, do you have a healthy relationship with money? When thinking about the dangers of loving money, keep in mind that it

- leads to sin

- hurts others

- ruins and destroys

- requires repentance

Do you view money correctly in that you understand it is amoral, but every one of your purchases is moral or immoral? Learning how to honor God by spending money the way He desires is a lifelong process. Remember that He sees and appreciates your efforts to serve Him. He will equip you to handle your finances in ways that serve and glorify Him.

CHAPTER 5

Learning from a Rich Fool

Consider this important question Jesus asked: "What will it profit a man if he gains the whole world and forfeits his soul? Or what shall a man give in return for his soul?" (Matthew 16:26). Now of course we know the answer: It would profit us nothing to gain the world and lose our soul, so there is nothing we would give in exchange for it. But Jesus taught a parable about a rich fool who did just this: He gained what the world offered and lost his soul. Jesus concluded by saying, "So is the one who lays up treasure for himself and is not rich toward God" (Luke 12:21).

With these words, Jesus moved from describing the rich fool to describing anyone who is earthly rich and heavenly poor. Let's consider the important lessons we can learn from the rich fool so that we avoid making any of the mistakes he made.

[The rich fool] didn't understand the concept of stewardship...and that anything he had ultimately belonged to God and was meant to be used for His glory.

The rich fool's harvest (essentially his wealth) became a problem for him. Are there any ways in which your wealth is a problem for you? Explain your answer.

EVERYTHING COMES FROM GOD

Name three things that were not mentioned in the chapter that are harder to be viewed as coming from God.

Name three things that were not mentioned in the chapter that are easier to be viewed as coming from God.

What are two other good answers the rich fool could have come up with to the question he asked about storing his crops?

WISE IN THE WORLD'S EYES, BUT FOOLS TO GOD

It's ironic that a man could look so wise and be called a fool.

In your own words, why do you think the rich fool would look wise in the world's eyes?

Name three things, financially speaking, we can do to ensure we look good in God's eyes.

The Rich Man Was a Fool Because He Didn't Give

-----

*God does not bless us so we can spend our fortunes on
ourselves. He blesses us so we can be a blessing to others.*

How did the rich man's use of personal pronouns reveal his perspective on life?

The rich fool was selfish with his crops. Name three ways it is easy to be tempted
to be selfish with your possessions.

Please answer the two questions from the chapter: Are you generous? Do you
use what God has blessed you with to bless others? Explain your answer.

The Rich Man Was a Fool Because He Didn't Plan for Eternity

-----

*When people are not living for the Lord, the best scenario for them is
to receive the news that they don't have much time left so they can be
shaken from their spiritual slumber and consider their eternal destiny.*

Describe the irony (or ironies) in the rich fool's life.

What we plan for reveals our focus and priorities. What do your plans reveal
about your priorities?

How does James 1:9-11 describe the reality of the rich who are caught up in their pursuits? Is there any exception for those who live for themselves?

Do we believe our soul could be required of us tonight, or do we believe—perhaps wrongly—that we have years left?

Discuss three ways you are preparing for eternity.

Discuss three ways you could better prepare for eternity.

The Rich Man Was a Fool Because He Didn't Know to Whom His Soul Belonged

What did the rich fool lose? You could say all his wealth and possessions, which is true, but he also lost something infinitely more important, and that's his soul.

How did the rich man's misunderstanding of his accountability to God for his soul influence the way he lived and managed his resources?

Please answer the questions from the chapter: do you…

recognize God owns you, including your soul?

understand you're going to be called to give an account for what you've done with the life God has given you?

The Rich Man Was a Fool Because He Wasn't Rich Toward God

People can look wise and successful in the world's eyes, but they can be fools and failures in God's eyes.

What does it mean to be rich toward God?

Do you think you are, or aren't, rich toward God? Explain your answer.

What ought we to consider when we are blessed by God with an abundance of material things?

Describe three things we can learn from the churches of Smyrna and Laodicea.

What evidences of God's grace were in the rich fool's life that he should have been aware of, and that should have caused him to think about God prior to the day of judgment?

WHAT MONEY CAN'T DO

Money can buy a vehicle, house, or even a person's loyalty for a while, but there are also many things even the richest people can't buy.

Why do you think money can't buy peace, righteousness, friendships, and a good reputation?

Describe three other important things in life that money can't buy.

WHAT THE GOSPEL CAN DO

His grace has the glorious effect of producing obedience in every area of life, including the handling of our finances.

What similarities do you see between yourself and the rich fool?

What differences do you see between yourself and the rich fool?

What relationship does the gospel have to the management of our finances?

We know Jesus wanted us to glean lessons from the fictional rich fool because He taught an entire parable about him. We can learn from the rich fool's example by keeping in mind what got him in trouble:

- He didn't give

- He didn't plan for eternity

- He didn't know who owned his soul

- He was spiritually poor

The chapter concluded with a discussion of the gospel's work in our lives. First, this should spur us to do what's right with our finances because of all that has been done for us. Second, thinking about the gospel's power should encourage us that we can grow and change. Conclude by asking God to help you in the stewardship of your finances.

CHAPTER 6

How to Avoid Being a Rich Fool

We have learned that being rich is not sinful or immoral. We have also learned about the rich fool, including how to avoid making the same mistakes he made. If there's nothing wrong with being rich, then the question is, How can we avoid being rich fools ourselves? What must we do to manage our finances God's way if we are wealthy?

We will learn practical answers to this question. It's not enough to simply not want to be like the rich fool. Because wisdom is the opposite of foolishness, we must take deliberate steps to do, with our money, *the opposite* of what he did with his money.

> *If we want to hear "Well done, good and faithful servant," we don't wait until the end of our lives to start being faithful.*

How have you started planning for the future?

Financially speaking, what decisions are you making now so that you can later hear, "Well done, good and faithful servant"?

THE RICH HAVE GREATER ACCOUNTABILITY

Stewardship is more difficult with more
money because there is more to steward.

Why does Paul criticize those who desire to be rich, but not those who are rich?

Why do the rich have greater accountability?

First, the Rich Should Be Humble (Versus Proud)

Keeping in mind that we have what we do only because
God provided it leaves no room for haughtiness.

Why is it tempting for the rich to look down on those who do not have as much?

Why doesn't money make rich people better (or worse) than those without riches?

Why is it important to recognize that God is the one who blesses us with material gain, and how should we respond to this recognition?

How can having riches deceive us into thinking our worth is found in something other than Christ?

Second, the Rich Should Trust God (Versus Their Riches)

Many people will tell you that putting confidence in their bank accounts left them terribly disappointed.

How can riches cause us to be self-reliant, and why is this dangerous?

Why is it tempting to rely on riches rather than God?

How does having riches give us a false confidence of being in control?

How does the mindset of being in control through riches affect our view of eternity?

Third, the Rich Should Do Good Works (Versus Only Give)

----

*Rich people have greater potential for acts of service—
their wealth provides them with the ability to do things
people with less money might not be able to do.*

Why is it wrong to think that good works can be substituted with financial giving?

Name three other things rich people might be tempted to pay for that God might want them to do themselves.

Fourth, the Rich Should Give Generously (Versus Stingily)

----

*We know from the parable of the talents in
chapter 1 that some are given more talents (wealth)
than others, and God expects more from them.*

Why should the rich "be generous and ready to share"?

What do and don't the words "take hold of eternal life" mean?

Rich people tend to have strong foundations for their lives on this side of heaven, but how can they ensure they have a strong foundation for the next life as well?

Give Generously Because You Can't Take It with You

> *We don't know exactly where our wealth will go; we just know it won't go with us.*

Why do you think God repeatedly reminds us that we can't take anything with us when this life comes to an end?

To make giving easier, what can you repeatedly tell yourself?

Give Generously to Send Wealth Ahead

> *How tragic that some people work so hard to prepare for the final years of this life but neglect the eternity that follows!*

What can we do with our money to have eternal treasure?

What are the two choices we face with our money?

Give Generously Because You Enjoy Riches for Only a Short Time

---

*The Christian life must be lived by
keeping the shortness of it in view.*

For the following three questions, follow Jonathan Edwards's example and write three resolutions you can commit to practice for God's glory:

Resolution one:

Resolution two:

Resolution three:

Why does God want us to focus on the shortness of this life?

How can the account of Daniel and Belshazzar encourage you to manage your finances God's way?

A BETTER APPROACH TO GIVING

With God's help—with the Spirit's enablement—we can manage our finances well, and even enjoy giving!

Why isn't simply trying to be a generous person the best approach to giving?

What can you begin telling yourself now that will make it easier to apply the following chapters on giving?

Often changing our behavior takes more time than going through one chapter of a book. Some of the things you are reading and learning about will compel you to adjust the way you handle your finances. But because change takes time, give yourself the weeks and months (versus hours and days) you might need. Don't be discouraged if things don't become more ideal overnight.

As you strive to manage your finances God's way, pray that He would give you the grace to do the things that He is revealing to you through your answers. Be sure to give thanks to God for the money that He has entrusted to you for your good and His glory.

CHAPTER 7

Give Willingly

Y ou must give ten percent!" You have probably heard this your whole Christian life. We know this designation came from the Old Testament when God commanded His people to give ten percent of their income. Or did He? What if I told you He actually commanded the Israelites to give two-and-a-half times that much? But even if He commanded people under the Old Covenant to give ten percent, is that what He commands us, the church, under the New Covenant? No, it's not.

Because the teaching about giving ten percent is so common, this might be one of the most difficult chapters for you to embrace. So, as I asked in the book, will you make a commitment right now to embrace what God's Word says even if it conflicts with a long-held and even popular teaching?

---

*Keep in mind how much God has done
for you so you're moved to give out of a heart
of worship versus out of duty.*

What have you previously been taught about how much to give?

Can you think of any New Testament verses that support giving ten percent, or any amount, for that matter? If yes, please list them. If not, why do you think there aren't any?

THE NEW TESTAMENT DOESN'T COMMAND GIVING A TITHE

The tithe was God's way of paying the priests who served God's people all throughout the Old Testament era up through the time of Jesus's earthly life.

The Mosaic law is associated with which covenant, and which mediator?

The law of Christ is associated with which covenant, and which mediator?

Two Categories of Commands

One fact that might surprise many people is God didn't even command giving a tithe in the Mosaic law. He commanded giving multiple tithes.

Describe the moral commands in the Mosaic law.

Describe the ceremonial commands in the Mosaic law.

Why are we unable to apply the command to tithe today like Israel could in the Old Testament?

A Higher Standard for Giving

*Because the law of Christ raised the bar in these areas,
we can conclude that it raised the bar for giving too.*

In what ways did Jesus raise the bar when He preached the Sermon on the Mount?

Why shouldn't ten percent be seen as the standard for Christians in the church?

No Mention of Tithing in the New Testament

*The epistles are the instruction letters for New Covenant believers
(those under the law of Christ), but there's no mention of giving a tithe.*

Why does God want us to give willingly versus out of obligation?

THE NEW TESTAMENT EXPECTS GIVING WILLINGLY

---

*We're not supposed to give because of external pressure,
such as the demands of others. When giving is done this
way, it resembles taxation more than worship.*

How does giving willingly show our worship?

What are some wrong ways for people to be encouraged to give?

How did Paul encourage the Corinthians to give?

WE MUST DECIDE HOW MUCH TO GIVE

No one can tell you how much to give, and that includes your pastor.

Why would God want us to be thoughtful about our giving as opposed to simply giving according to a percentage?

How can you go about deciding how much to give?

GOD SEES THE "HEART GIFT" VERSUS THE "HAND GIFT"

Describe a "heart gift."

Describe a "hand gift."

GIVING WILLINGLY IN THE OLD TESTAMENT

Giving willingly is elevated, while giving reluctantly causes suffering.

Why did God want His people to give a tithe in the Old Testament?

How did God encourage giving willingly in the Old Testament?

How does a freewill offering show the motive of the heart better than giving by compulsion?

Jacob Demonstrates Giving Unwillingly

It's hard to imagine any spiritual benefit for the giver when the giving is done reluctantly versus willingly.

Are there any ways you try to manipulate God like Jacob did? Explain your answer.

Do you think God should bless us when we give unwillingly? Why or why not?

Abraham Demonstrates Giving Willingly

[Abraham] gave like a New Covenant believer under the Old Covenant!

How did Abraham and Jacob give differently?

How is Abraham's giving of a tithe different than the giving of a tithe as commanded by the Mosaic law?

THANKFULNESS PRODUCES BETTER GIVING THAN LAW

Giving out of thankfulness is superior to giving out of obligation.

Why do thankful hearts always give more than hearts giving out of obligation?

Can you think of any other examples in Scripture of giving willingly and with a thankful heart?

JESUS WILLINGLY GAVE MORE THAN A TITHE

Instead of giving us 10 or 25 percent,
Jesus gave us 100 percent.

How is Jesus the ultimate example of giving willingly?

In what other ways did the Old Testament sacrifices and offerings look forward to Christ?

Although we can't approach what Christ gave for us, what can we give in response to what we have been given?

SO WHY GIVE WILLINGLY?

We give because we're thankful. What an incredible gift God
has given us in being able to worship Him this way!

In your own words, how does Jesus's sacrifice encourage you to give willingly versus under compulsion or out of obligation?

Think about how willingly Jesus gave of Himself. How could this not encourage us to give willingly in response? We don't give to be saved or earn favor with God. We give because we are saved, and it's an act of worship born from a thankful heart.

Should you finish this chapter and recognize that you don't want to give as willingly as you know you should, pray that God increases your thankfulness. Maybe you still find generosity to be a struggle. If so, it's good for you to have the humility to recognize this weakness. In response, pray that God helps you to grow in this area, recognizing that He wants you to have a heart of worship.

CHAPTER 8

Give Sacrificially

———

Sometimes what we really need to be motivated is a good example. We see what others have done and we are encouraged, challenged, and convicted. The apostle Paul hoped the Macedonians' example in giving (despite their poverty) would do just that for the Corinthians. But not only were the Macedonians a picture of sacrificial giving for the Corinthians, they are a great example for us as well.

The Macedonians reveal why sacrifice in giving is so important, and how wonderfully God can stretch our giving beyond what we would expect. We will see that not only does God look at the amount we give, He also looks at the commitment behind it.

Giving is much bigger than the gift.

Share about a gift you received that was meaningful not because of the gift itself, but because of the sacrifice behind it.

Just as the Macedonians' giving served as an example to the Corinthians, describe someone whose giving has served as an example to you.

THE MACEDONIANS—A GREAT EXAMPLE FOR THE CORINTHIANS AND US

The Macedonians are a good example of the poor and afflicted giving generously too.

What circumstances were the Macedonians in when they gave?

Why do you think the Macedonians weren't deterred from giving despite their circumstances?

During trials, what can we tell ourselves so that we continue to think about others versus only thinking about ourselves?

What do you think led the Macedonians to "give beyond their means"?

Do you think we should "give beyond our means"? Explain your answer.

A Poor Widow's Giving

Jesus wasn't just watching what people gave; He was watching how, or in what way, they gave.

Why do you think Jesus was watching how people gave versus how much they gave?

In what way did the widow, who gave a small amount, give more than everyone else?

An Example of Eternal Rewards

*The widow had no idea Jesus was watching her,
just as we easily forget that the Lord is watching us.*

How did the widow give so little on earth, but deposit so much in heaven?

Why God Cares About the Sacrifice Versus the Amount

*The amount we give isn't of greatest importance
to God because He doesn't need our money.*

If God doesn't need our money, why do you think—in your own words—He still wants us to give?

Our Sacrifice Is Worship

We worship by offering ourselves as living sacrifices.

Why should the word *worship* cause us to think of sacrifice?

Sacrificial Worship with Abraham and Isaac

How were Abraham and Isaac *both* worshipping in Genesis 22?

Sacrificial Worship with Animals

Why did God repeatedly ask for animals that were "without blemish"?

Sacrificial Worship with David

David wouldn't offer anything to the Lord that cost him nothing.

How did David reveal that he understood worship must involve sacrifice?

Giving Without Sacrifice

While I can't say how much we should give,
I can say this: it must involve sacrifice.

In your own words, why do you think giving without sacrifice is not worshipful?

Give According to Your Income

God doesn't set a fixed percentage, but He does
expect the amount to be relative to our income.

Assuming you give a tithe or ten percent, would you consider making it a matter of prayer and thoughtful consideration to determine an amount to give that is according to your income? Explain your answer.

Giving in America

Most people in the rest of the world would
love to prosper "as little as we do."

Why do you think Americans give as little as they do despite their prosperity?

If we aren't giving much, what does that say about our hearts?

Prefigured in the Old Testament

-----

*The Old Testament foreshadows the New Testament,
and this is true about giving according to our income.*

Even though people were commanded to give a tithe in the Old Testament, why do you think there were still times God expected His people to give according to their income?

Considering God expects us to give according to our income, what changes do you need to make to your giving? Be specific, if possible.

The "Gift" of Giving

So, is giving a gift or command? Both!

What gifts do you believe God has given you? If you are unfamiliar with the gifts, read the three key passages listing them: Romans 12:6-8; 1 Corinthians 12:4-11; and 1 Peter 4:10-11.

Can you think of other gifts that are also commanded of believers?

Why does God command us to give even if we don't have the gift of giving?

Giving isn't easy! If giving feels easy to us, we might not be giving enough. The good news is that the harder it is to give—the more sacrifice that's involved—the more worshipful it is to God.

Some people would rather do almost anything else than give money. That, in and of itself, is not necessarily wrong. It is only wrong if they give in to the temptation not to give. If you find it extraordinarily difficult to give sacrificially and according to your income, pray that God helps you to be more generous and worshipful. Keep in mind that He wants you to be able to give in a way that pleases Him.

CHAPTER 9

God's Generosity Encourages Giving Cheerfully

The Macedonians were wonderful givers, but they pale in comparison to God. He is the ultimate Giver. His kindness should lead us to give to Him and others. God gives to us for this very reason, that we might be generous in response. But God is so good that as we give (or sow) we will often find ourselves receiving (reaping).

This allows us to do something that might seem contradictory: give sacrificially *and* cheerfully. If you still find it difficult to give cheerfully as you work your way through this chapter, I have three encouragements for you at the end.

Because God gives, giving is righteous and makes us imitators of Him.

How is God the ultimate example of giving?

List five wonderful blessings God has given you.

GOD GIVES TO US SO WE CAN GIVE TO OTHERS

We should do for others what God has done for us.

What are three things God has done for you that you have, in turn, done for others?

In what ways does God give gifts differently than us?

REAPING AND SOWING

If a farmer planted only a few seeds because he wanted to retain as much as possible, he would have more seed in his sacks, but at harvest time, he would have less grain in his barn.

What does it mean that we reap what we sow?

Name three areas of life to which the principle of sowing and reaping applies.

With the understanding that parables put physical stories alongside spiritual truths, describe the spiritual truths learned from two different parables.

If We Give Enough Will God Make Us Rich?

_____

*We don't give to receive, but God wants us to know that
He doesn't ask that we give ourselves into poverty.*

_____

Will God always give us more than we have given? Why or why not?

What are the differences between needs and wants?

List three needs and three wants.

Do We Reap in This Life or the Next?

_____

*God is going to reward us with far more
than what we have done for Him.*

_____

Does giving benefit us in this life, the next life, or both? Explain your answer.

How does God ensure we don't outgive Him?

GOD GIVES US GRACE SO WE CAN GIVE MORE

[God's] infinite amount of grace allows Him to dispense it to us lavishly.

How could the Macedonians give so much when they were so poor?

Name three ways God could bless us so we can give more.

GIVE CHEERFULLY

---

*A gift, regardless of what it is, means so
much more when given cheerfully.*

Share a time someone gave to you cheerfully, and describe how it made you feel.

Share a time someone gave to you sorrowfully, and describe how it made you feel.

How can we give sacrificially and cheerfully?

Putting God First

The Macedonians demonstrate that if we put God first, not only will we give the amount He wants, we will give the way He wants—cheerfully.

Why did the Macedonians give to the Lord first before giving of their means?

What does it look like to put God first?

What is the relationship between giving and worry? In other words, why might Jesus preach about not worrying immediately after preaching about giving?

A Wonderful Reason to Give Cheerfully

God loves everyone, but He has a special, unique love for cheerful givers.

Why do you think God loves cheerful givers?

How Do Parents Want Their Children to Give?

―――――――

*We take pleasure in [our children's] gifts
because they're signs of their love for us.*

―――――――

If you're a parent, how do you want your children to give you gifts? How do you *not* want them to give you gifts? If you don't have children, then do your best to guess what you would desire and dislike when your children give you gifts.

Provide an example of giving grudgingly.

Provide an example of giving out of duty.

Provide an example of giving out of thanks.

GIVE WITH THE RIGHT HEART

―――――――

*We are giving with the right heart when it's enough
to know that He sees and will reward us.*

―――――――

Why does our heart matter when giving?

What does it look like when we give with a right heart?

What does it look like when we give with a wrong heart?

THREE ENCOURAGEMENTS FOR GIVING

If you're an American, do you think it is strange that we need to be encouraged to give despite how wealthy we are?

Encouragement One: Confession and Prayer

*Ask [God] to replace your unwillingness with willingness,
your joylessness with joyfulness, your cheerlessness
with cheerfulness, your stinginess with generosity,
and your wrong heart with a right heart.*

Write out, word for word, a prayer asking God to help you give joyfully, cheerfully, generously, and with the right heart.

Encouragement Two: Scripture Memorization and Meditation

Choose three verses that will help you be a better giver and write them on note cards.

Where will you put these note cards, and how often you will read them?

Encouragement Three: Reflection on God's Greatest Gift

———————————

*Giving is the appropriate response from people
who realize how much they've been given.*

———————————

Describe three things God has given you that encourage you to give in response.

Write three things you can say to yourself to encourage you to give when you find it difficult to do so.

As you grow in your relationship with Christ, you will develop greater affection for Him and thankfulness for what He has given you. The natural byproduct of this thankfulness will be a desire to give in return. You are not saved by what you do for God. You do not increase your standing with Him by anything you could do. Instead, your standing with Him is established by what Christ has done for you. This giving is sacrificial, worshipful, and initiated by God's generosity.

Some days you won't feel like giving, which is to say you won't feel like worshipping. On those days, revisit the three encouragements and the notes and verses you have written to help you imitate God, the ultimate Giver.

CHAPTER 10

Good Stewardship Toward the Poor

B y now we have learned how important it is to be generous. Giving is one of the most important aspects of financial stewardship. But we know we can't give to every need. Not only do we not have the money to do so, there are times when giving hurts more than it helps. Typically, this is the case with those who are lazy.

Making this more difficult is God's concern for the poor and less fortunate. So we find ourselves in a dilemma: We know God wants us to help others, but at the same time, there are those whom we should not help. Part of being a good steward is knowing when to say, "I should not give in this situation." Fortunately, God's Word gives us the knowledge we need to know when to give and when not to give.

Saying yes to something means saying no to something else in most areas of life, but it is especially true when our resources are limited, such as time and money.

Define laziness.

As you get to know families, what are three signs that they might struggle with laziness?

Describe three ways to help those affected by unfortunate circumstances, such as economic downturns or unexpected medical issues, while still giving them a sense of purpose.

Describe three ways to help those who are suffering because of poor choices or laziness.

Do you know anyone who wants to be working but isn't or is in between jobs? What could you do to help them find work—such as tell them about a job you're aware of, or invite them to work with your family?

A BETTER APPROACH TO CHARITY

Our government gives people handouts that require little more than standing in line or walking to a mailbox to collect a check.

What are some of the negative consequences of a welfare system that requires little of the recipients?

What do you think could be done to improve our welfare system?

Briefly describe God's welfare system under the Mosaic law.

Can you think of any other reasons God's welfare system is better than what we see done by the government?

In what ways does Ruth serve as a good example for us?

A COMMAND VERSUS SUGGESTION

*If we should keep away from people who call themselves
Christians but are idle or lazy, it is hard to imagine
that God would expect us to give them money.*

Why do you think God commanded, versus suggested or recommended, that we avoid the lazy?

Has your mindset toward the lazy changed at all after reading what Paul commanded? If so, how?

A GOOD EXAMPLE TO FOLLOW

*All Christians should see themselves as examples
through whom others see Christ.*

Mention three ways Paul was a good example to follow.

Describe three people who have been good examples for you to follow.

As Christians, why must we strive to be good examples to others, whether they are believers or unbelievers?

GOOD STEWARDS SUPPORT THEIR CHURCH LEADERS

*One of the nice things about giving to your church is the
elders or church leadership can then determine the best
uses of the money, such as paying the pastor(s), supporting
ministries and missionaries, and handling benevolence.*

Why should church leaders be supported by their congregations?

In what ways, not just financially, do you support your church leaders?

Why do you think so many church leaders are overworked and underpaid?

Why might it be better to simply give to your church and allow the leaders to handle benevolence, versus trying to handle benevolence yourself?

DISTINGUISHING BETWEEN TWO GROUPS

The words "will not work" allow us to distinguish between two completely different groups: those unable to work and those unwilling to work.

Describe three benevolence issues that can be entrusted to church leaders.

Describe three benevolence issues that can't be handed over to church leaders.

Good Stewards Give to Those Unable to Work

These passages reveal just how important it is to care for those in need.

Describe three legitimate situations that prevent people from working.

Describe three illegitimate situations that prevent people from working.

Why do you think it is so important to God for us to help those in need?

Poor Stewards Give to Those Unwilling to Work

As important as it is to give to those who through no fault of their own find themselves struggling financially, it is equally important to avoid giving to those who through fault of their own find themselves struggling financially.

Why would giving to every need make us poor stewards of our finances?

Why is enablement unloving?

Why is it so important to avoid giving to those who are unwilling to work, or to those who have given in to the temptation to be lazy?

What can we do to determine whether people are unwilling or unable to work?

What things can you do to keep busy when you are tempted to be lazy?

Detriment One: Wastes Money

I'm left wondering how much better of a steward I might have been if I had given that same money to one of our missionaries instead.

Why doesn't giving money typically help people spiritually?

What is the best way to help people spiritually?

Detriment Two: Hinders Repentance

How much damage would've been done if well-meaning people "helped" the prodigal son?

What can it look like when those who are unwilling to work experience the consequences of their actions?

Why does giving to those unwilling to work hinder their repentance?

Detriment Three: Enables Further Sin

———————

Idleness breeds compromise and is a foundation for other sins.

———————

How does idleness typically lead to other sins?

Detriment Four: Prevents Shame

———————

*Shame can only be produced by the knowledge
that you have done something wrong.*

———————

Why is it good to experience shame?

What allows us to experience shame?

What prevents us from experiencing shame?

KEEP DOING GOOD

———————

*It is easy to become cynical, stop giving, and neglect the genuinely
needy just because some people are not willing to work.*

———————

When lazy people around you are not working, how can you discipline yourself to remain diligent in your workplace?

In what ways are you encouraged when others around you are working?

The greatest reason for us to help those in need is God helped us when we were in need. Romans 5:8 says, "God shows his love for us in that while we were still sinners, Christ died for us." While we were sinning and in rebellion against God, He loved us and saved us. He became a man in the person of Jesus Christ. Then He was willing to die on a cross in our place and take the punishment that our sins deserve. This same God expects us, as His followers, to help others in need.

But at the same time, God doesn't want us to enable people to continue in sin. Not only does it not help, it actually hurts them. Our generosity can be detrimental because we might hinder repentance, enable further sin, or prevent the shame that should be experienced. Clearly wisdom is required to know when to give. Pray God gives you this wisdom so you can manage your finances in ways that please Him.

CHAPTER 11

Spending Problems Versus an Income Problem

W e want to have the money to give, save, and buy the things we need. When we want to give, save, or buy more than we already do, we typically think in terms of finding ways to increase our income. We hope for a raise, look for a second job, or put in overtime. These are all ways to get more money. But what if, instead of working harder to acquire more money, we made decisions that allowed the money we have to go that much farther? In other words, what if we could give more, save more, and buy more by spending less?

This approach works because most people have spending problems versus income problems. In this chapter, we are going to talk about the ways we can make our income go farther with some wise decisions.

> *Most people throughout history*
> *have wanted necessities, but the more common*
> *problem today is having too much stuff.*

SPENDING PROBLEMS OFTEN RESULT FROM SMALL PURCHASES THAT ADD UP

Imagine what happens when you add up all the other small purchases, such as eating out or grabbing that extra item at the store that you don't really need.

What are some reasons our small purchases add up quickly without us giving them a second thought?

What are two excuses you regularly tell yourself to justify small purchases that add up?

What are three small purchases you make on a regular basis that can be eliminated from your expenditures?

SPENDING PROBLEMS OFTEN RESULT FROM WORTHLESS PURCHASES

If the item is valuable at the moment but it has no value to us in the future, it has been a worthless purchase.

What are three worthless purchases you have made in the last year?

What can you do to avoid making worthless purchases in the future?

SPENDING PROBLEMS OFTEN RESULT FROM SELF-ENTITLEMENT

What are three ways the Old Testament benefits us?

Eve's Entitlement

The devil tried to make Eve feel entitled, and it worked.

What most often causes you to feel entitled?

Amnon's Entitlement

Describe a time a friend made you feel entitled to buy something, including what the friend said to you.

King Ahab's Entitlement

Jezebel made Ahab feel so entitled that he murdered Naboth and took his vineyard.

Describe a time a family member, such as a spouse, parent, or child, made you feel entitled to buy something, including what the person said to you.

Beware of Self-Entitlement from Any Source

Many people are in debt, with little savings, simply because of these three little words: "I deserve this."

In your life, are you the person most likely to make you feel entitled through the things you tell yourself? Explain your answer.

SPENDING PROBLEMS OFTEN RESULT FROM IMPATIENCE

Scripture calls us to be patient and informs us of patience's several benefits.

What are two benefits of patience?

When it comes to purchases, why is patience so important?

Don't Be an Esau!

Esau was impatient and it caused him regret, and we,
too, can be impatient in ways that lead us to regret.

Describe a time you were dramatic to justify a purchase—a time you said, "I have to have this…" when you didn't really have to have it.

Describe two times you've regretted purchases.

Why do you think the patient children in the Stanford marshmallow experiment were so much more successful later in life?

Wait Two (or More) Weeks

Often when people experience regret, it occurs within a few days.

Describe two purchases you made that you regretted that you probably would not have made if you had waited two weeks.

SPENDING PROBLEMS OFTEN RESULT FROM MISUNDERSTANDING "GOOD DEALS"

Have you ever noticed that whenever you want to buy something, regardless of the season of the year or your geographic location, you are able to find a "good deal"?

Discuss three times you thought you were getting a good deal, but in hindsight, you realized that wasn't the case.

HOW DO WE KNOW WHEN TO SPEND MONEY?

How do you currently decide when to spend money?

First, Do Your Research

If you're unfamiliar with the average prices of the item you're considering buying, then how will you know if you should make the purchase or keep looking?

Think of three upcoming purchases you will need to make, and answer the following two questions.

Who do you know that is knowledgeable and can be consulted as you do your research to ensure you make a good purchase?

What are three websites, books, are other resources you can use to help you make a good purchase?

Second, Let God's Commands Serve as Fleeces

———

When we look at what God's Word says about debt, family, marriage, children, pride, covetousness, entitlement, selfishness, materialism—and the list could go on—we have enough information to make the right decisions with purchases (and most other areas of life).

———

Think of two major purchases you must make in the future and then answer the following questions:

What are three commands in God's Word that can help direct you as you make the purchases?

What are three questions you can ask yourself that can help direct you as you make the purchases?

What three sinful motivations will you need to resist that could cause you to make the wrong purchases?

An Example from Our Lives

———————

*We felt thankful that we didn't compromise on one of
the fleeces and possibly miss out on God's best.*

———————

Can you think of an example from your life when God's commands served as fleeces to determine His will? If yes, explain. If not, share about a time God's commands *should have* served as fleeces to determine His will.

JESUS'S EXAMPLE

———————

*To increase our motivation to obey the teaching in this
chapter, we need look no further than our Savior.*

———————

How does Jesus's example motivate you to want to obey God's commands?

Jesus's Self-Denial

———————

We will have victory over self-entitlement when we obey Jesus's words.

———————

How can Jesus's example of self-denial help us deny ourselves and resist the temptation to be entitled?

Jesus's Patience

---

*The difference between Jesus and Esau is Jesus resisted
the temptation to be impulsive...As Jonadab and Esau
show us what not to do, Jesus shows us what to do.*

How can Jesus's example of patience help us be patient when it comes to purchases?

Self-entitlement has caused people many financial problems. As we learn to resist this temptation and apply the principles in this chapter, such as doing our research, being patient, and allowing God's commandments to serve as fleeces for us, we will be protecting ourselves against poor financial decisions that later lead to regret.

We should be "looking to Jesus, the founder and perfecter of our faith, who for the joy that was set before him endured the cross, despising the shame" (Hebrews 12:2). As we consider His examples of self-denial and patience, we can be encouraged to follow in His steps. Conclude this chapter by praying that the Father will help you be like His Son.

CHAPTER 12

God's View of Debt

M y wife, Katie, and I had our ninth child at the time I was writing this. We didn't set out to have lots of children (although we are unspeakably blessed by each of them). We simply wanted—and to be clear, this is not a commentary on others who have taken a different approach—God to create our family for us, and we thought the best way to do that was to let Him give us children as He saw fit. He could have given us fewer, and He could still give us more, but we wanted to reach the end of our lives and feel like we had the children He wanted us to have. One of the main reasons we feel this way is that, in Scripture, we see children presented as blessings.

We would never want to be wrong about what God says is a blessing or a curse. The number of abortions performed each year reveal many people think children are curses instead of blessings. Similarly, the amount of debt people (and countries) have reveals debt is viewed as a blessing. But God's Word presents debt as something to be avoided. Regardless of what you may have thought about debt previously, let's take an honest look at what Scripture says about it.

We think debt is a blessing because it allows us
to buy things with money we don't have.

Have your actions shown that you view debt as a blessing or as something to avoid?

As you begin this chapter, what can you do to ensure you embrace God's view of debt, even if it conflicts with any previous view you've had?

GOD'S VIEW OF DEBT

To learn the Bible's teaching on debt, we must understand the difference between law and wisdom literature.

Describe the difference(s) between law and wisdom.

The Law and Debt

The law does not condemn lending and borrowing.

What does the law condemn?

Wisdom and Debt

*Combining the teaching on debt from the law and wisdom
literature, we find the biblical balance is this: Because debt is
not forbidden in the law it is not necessarily sinful, but because
wisdom warns against it, we are wise to try to avoid it.*

How does debt make people slaves?

Why do you think Christians are willing to embrace debt too easily even though the Bible warns against it?

EVEN CHURCHES CAN BE WRONG

*We shouldn't be surprised when the world acts like debt is a
blessing, but we should be surprised when churches act like
debt is a blessing and hold a view contradictory to God's Word.*

Why is it even worse for churches to go into debt than it is for individual Christians to go into debt?

Describe what churches could do to avoid debt.

DEBT IS YOUR ENEMY VERSUS YOUR FRIEND

---

*As a pastor, I have watched debt cause enough problems
that it would be unloving of me not to warn you.*

Describe three situations that have the potential to put people in debt for legitimate reasons.

Why does debt (wrongly) seem like your friend?

Why is debt your enemy versus your friend?

OUR NATION'S DEBT

Why do we have a debt ceiling if we keep raising it?

Why do you think our nation takes on debt recklessly?

Biting the Bullet

---

*Suffer through difficult years, including economic slowdowns,
and lower the quality of living until the debt is in check.*

Do you see any other ways to lower our nation's debt?

Why does a nation crumble when people learn they can vote themselves the greatest amount of immediate prosperity?

Sacrificing Our Children's Future for Our Present

We have an amazing capacity to sacrifice the future
for the present, but what's surprising is we will even
sacrifice our children's future for the present.

Why do you think otherwise loving people can find themselves tempted to sacrifice their children's future for their present?

The Bible's Condemnation

Most Americans don't spend or view debt any
differently than the government.

Why are American citizens at least partly responsible for the foolish financial decisions government officials make?

INDIVIDUAL DEBT

Write out the total amount of your debt. Keep this in mind for when you fill out your budget.

Credit Card Debt

Embracing credit card debt is one of the worst financial mistakes we make.

Why is credit card debt so financially devastating?

Write out all your credit card debt.

Automobile Debt

New vehicles are one of the worst investments people make, yet plenty of people still purchase them.

Why is embracing automobile debt such a poor financial decision?

Why is it better to purchase a used car versus a new one?

Write out all your automobile debt.

Student Loan Debt

———————————

*How many graduates can say the money they made
from their degrees exceeded the money they could've
made if that same amount were invested?*

———————————

What do you think has contributed to the student loan crisis in the United States?

Misconception One: A Degree Always Improves Your Life

Why do you think so many people regret taking out student loans and even regret going to college altogether?

Misconception Two: You Need a Degree to Succeed

———————————

*Those who work in other professions, such as firefighters,
insurance agents, cooks, plumbers, exterminators, medical
assistants, landscapers, construction workers, and
phlebotomists, don't need degrees, and some of these jobs
pay as much or more than those requiring degrees.*

———————————

Why do you think so many people believe they must have a degree to succeed?

Misconception One: You Must Go into Debt to Get a Degree

What are three practical strategies people could follow to avoid going into debt when getting a degree? For example, living with parents versus living on campus.

Mortgage Debt

When people have a mortgage, unless they are close to paying it off, they should not consider themselves close to being debt-free.

Why should you strive to pay off your mortgage?

How much is your mortgage?

Why can it be unwise to view a home as an investment that will appreciate?

TRUST GOD TO HELP YOU

If you are a Christian, you are God's child, and just like earthly parents want to see their children manage their finances well, our heavenly Father wants to see us manage our finances well.

Why should you be committed to getting out of debt?

Spiritually speaking, why can you be encouraged in your pursuit to be debt-free?

Few things are harder than embracing a truth that conflicts with something we have previously believed. That can be made even more difficult when those closest to us share the same wrong belief. We can be bombarded with poor counsel and overwhelmed with advice that conflicts with Scripture.

But as Christians, we must be guided by God's Word and committed to following it regardless of what we have previously believed, been taught, or seen take place around us. Debt is one of those challenging areas in which we find difficulty obeying God's Word. Pray that God will give you the grace and wisdom needed to practice the financial discipline that is strongly encouraged in Scripture.

CHAPTER 13

Avoiding and Eliminating Debt

N ow that we hopefully are committed to avoiding debt and paying off debt, we must figure out some good strategies for doing these things. The debt that understandably seems most unavoidable is a mortgage. Even people committed to being debt-free often feel like they can't be mortgage-free. So we will begin with some approaches to being able to purchase a home with cash.

After that, most of the rest of the chapter will focus on practical ways to save money. Any money that isn't spent can then be put toward paying off the debt you have, making future purchases with cash, saving more, and increasing your giving.

I have watched young and old people alike,
inside and outside my church,
purchase homes without mortgages.

Can you think of any testimonies of people who lived in ways the world would consider to be extreme so they could buy a house debt-free?

AVOIDING A MORTGAGE

First, Consider a Rental

The money going toward the interest isn't going toward the price of your house any more than rent goes toward the price of your house.

Why is it reasonable to live in a rental while saving up money to buy your house with cash?

Second, Live Modestly

Name three sacrifices you can make now to live more modestly and save money.

Third, Purchase a Starter Home

Who says you need to live in your dream home in your twenties or thirties?

Why might it be wise to first purchase a starter home versus your dream home?

If You Decide to Purchase a Mortgage

Understand "Qualifying"

> *Real estate agents and loan officers want you
> to sign for the most amount of money.*

What does (and doesn't) qualifying for a loan mean?

Choose A 15-Year Versus a 30-Year Mortgage

> *The only downside to a 15-year mortgage is larger
> monthly payments, but most people would be
> surprised to learn they're not that much larger.*

What are three things you can tell yourself to be encouraged to go with a 15-year versus a 30-year mortgage?

STRATEGIES TO ELIMINATE DEBT

Sacrifice

> *While formulas and budgeting techniques can be
> helpful, there's no substitute for sacrifice.*

Why would it be difficult for us to become debt-free if we are "normal" versus extreme? In other words, what changes do you need to make to live radically so you can pay off your debt as soon as possible?

Live Below Your Income

Once you create a budget, you will be able to come up with exact numbers, but for now, figure out your income. Then guess what amount below your income you can live off. Subtract that amount from your income, then multiply the difference times 12 to see how much you can save each year. What amount did you come up with? Are you surprised you can save this much? Explain your answer.

Eliminate Unnecessary Expenses

It may seem impossible to live without certain pleasures you've always enjoyed, but remember: The more expenses you eliminate, the faster you'll be out of debt.

List three to five expenses you can eliminate to save money.

Buy Used

When you need "new" stuff, you can spend a fraction of the price buying used.

Name three things you will need in the future that you can buy used instead of new.

Stay Home

First, Build Relationships

When your children feel connected to you and each other, they will be more interested in staying at home because this is where they can be with those who are closest to them.

What are two things you can do to build relationships between your family members?

Second, Avoid Conflict

What are two causes of conflict in your relationship with your spouse, or your children, or your parents, and what can you do to grow in these areas?

Third, Invest in Your Home

Discuss three investments you can make in your home to make it a more attractive place to spend time.

Avoid Lavishness

When eliminating debt, settle for simplicity.

Being aware of temptation ahead of time increases the chances of resisting it when it arises. What are three future purchases you will need to make for your home that will tempt you to be lavish or extravagant?

Avoid "Going Big"

A minimalist approach not only keeps expenses and expectations low, it also minimizes stress and covetousness.

What can you do (or avoid) for birthdays that will allow you to save money?

What can you do (or avoid) for holidays—in particular, Christmas—that will allow you to save money?

If you have children (or you expect to have them), what toys can you invest in that will save money and foster creativity?

Avoid Expensive Hobbies

What are three hobbies you can engage in that are inexpensive?

Enjoy Free

---

*Have you been led to believe that you must
spend money to enjoy yourself?*

What are three activities you can do that are free?

Keep the End in Mind

Why is it so important to keep the end in mind?

What can you dream about that will encourage you when you must make sacrifices?

Continue Giving

---

*If you want to honor God by paying off your debt, you
must also want to honor Him by continuing to give.*

Why is continuing to give a vital strategy to becoming debt-free?

PUT EXTRA MONEY TOWARD DEBT

-----

*When you receive your tax return, Christmas or
birthday cash, inheritance money, or income earned
on the side, put it toward debt repayment.*

Looking into the future, what are some extra sources of cash you might receive
that you can decide now you will put toward repaying your debt?

WHAT ABOUT WHEN YOU'RE OUT OF DEBT?

-----

*After we got out of debt, we made some purchases we wouldn't have
made if we were still in debt, but our lifestyles didn't change that much.*

Why shouldn't our lifestyles change that much after we are debt-free?

What would be some acceptable ways for our lifestyles, or our spending practices, to change after becoming debt-free?

What would be some unacceptable ways for our lifestyles, or our spending practices, to change after becoming debt-free?

POSSIBLY MISSING OUT ON GOD'S BEST

---

*If you buy something when you don't have the money
to do so, you might be missing these and other
wonderful blessings God has in store for you.*

If you do your best to put your spending choices in God's hands, why might the answer be *not yet* instead of *no*?

Why might you be missing out on God's best if you go forward with a purchase that isn't His will at the time?

Eliminating debt is difficult. It involves saying no to things we want, and often even saying no to things we have enjoyed, perhaps for much of our lives. But this type of sacrifice is required to be debt-free. Applying the strategies from this chapter, and any others the Holy Spirit reveals to you as you seek to manage your finances God's way, will put you on the path to financial freedom.

Remember to keep the end in mind. Not only will this give you the necessary diligence, but it will also allow you to begin experiencing some of the joy you will know when you pay off that last cent of debt. As you dream about what that day will be like, you will be able to avoid spending money that should be put toward eliminating debt.

CHAPTER 14

Saving the Right and Wrong Way

Even when doing good things in life—such as getting a job, improving our health, or finishing our education—there are good and bad ways to go about them. Saving money is no different. In this chapter, we will cover some good ways to go about accumulating money, and some ways that should be avoided.

To give you the necessary motivation to start saving early, I'll share some statistics about the numbers of people with financial regrets. I don't want you to be one of them! If you've never been a big saver—perhaps you've been a big spender—changing is difficult. I understand. Let's dig in together and see what God has to say to us through His Word.

We get into the habit of doing things one way and it's difficult to do things differently.

Describe three of your good habits.

Describe three of your bad habits.

What are three things you can do to try to change the bad habits you just listed?

WE DEVELOP THE HABIT OF SPENDING OR SAVING MONEY

We can't develop the habit of spending and
saving money. They are mutually exclusive.

Do you have a habit of spending money, or saving it? Explain your answer.

What are three things you can tell yourself to discourage you from spending money that should be saved?

Describe three things you can do to become excited about saving money.

THE BIBLE'S VIEW OF SAVING

Recognizing a coming need and preparing today
is wise. Doing so enables us to care for ourselves,
family members, friends, and neighbors.

Why do you think the Bible speaks so positively of saving?

Aside from Joseph, describe a person in the Bible who prepared well for the future, and how that preparation benefited others.

AVOIDING FINANCIAL REGRETS

One of the worst things to have to say is, "I wish I could go back and do things differently."

Why do you think so many people have so little money saved?

ACCUMULATING MONEY THE RIGHT WAY

We are being poor stewards when we waste money on trivial purchases, but we are also being poor stewards when we allow money to sit for years (or decades) without growing in value.

Why are the words *at once* so important?

In what areas of life are you most tempted to procrastinate, and what do you need to do to improve in these areas?

Taking Advantage of Time and Interest

———————————

*Time, versus money itself, is the greatest tool we
have to increase the value of money.*

———————————

Recognizing the importance of investing as early as possible, how much can you commit to investing per month? If you aren't sure yet, when you fill out your budget, you might be able to determine a more accurate number.

Contrast Peter and Paul

What steps do you need to take to ensure you are more like Paul and less like Peter?

Discuss three reasons people don't start saving and investing earlier.

ACCUMULATING MONEY WRONG WAYS

———————————

*Psalm 50:10 says God owns the cattle on a thousand hills. He has
no trouble providing for us when we obey Him with our finances.*

———————————

Why is it difficult to trust God with our finances?

What would it look like for you to trust God with your finances?

Avoid Gaining Money Corruptly

*Anything gained corruptly should be
viewed as cursed instead of blessed.*

Describe three ways you could be tempted to gain money corruptly.

When tempted to gain money corruptly, what are three encouragements you can give yourself to help resist this temptation?

Avoid Gaining Money Quickly

*The desire to obtain money quickly is
fueled by impatience and often laziness.*

When tempted to gain money quickly, what are three things you can tell yourself to resist this temptation?

What About Gambling?

---

*Everything in casinos is rigged to take money and give
nothing in return, except fleeting pleasures and regret.*

What are three things you can tell yourself when you're tempted to gamble?

Is the Stock Market Gambling?

---

*When investors buy stock, they obtain partial
ownership of a company to make money over time.*

In what ways do you think investing in the stock market is different than spending money in a casino?

TEACH YOUR CHILDREN TO SAVE

---

*If we save money, avoid debt, give, and make wise financial
decisions, we are teaching our children to do the same.*

Why is it so important for parents to teach their children to save?

What are three practical ways parents can teach their children to save?

Why is it so important for parents to set a good example to their children?

HELPED BY GOD

*Keep in mind that God is for you.
He wants you to make the right decisions with
the money He has entrusted to you.*

What are two other verses in Scripture that reveal God wants to help you obey Him?

Breaking bad habits and establishing new ones is challenging. When we have been doing something for years, but we want to do something different we must pray for the grace and resolve to change. Ask God to help you grow in any weak areas related to finances, whether spending too much, not saving enough, or failing to give as you should. Any time you sincerely try to correct a wrong action, God will notice your desire and bless your efforts. Why? Because God wants to see us walk in obedience.

Trust that the gospel is at work in your heart enabling you to manage your finances well. Keep in mind that as a faithful heavenly Father, God will always give you the amount of money He knows you need. It is then our responsibility to be faithful and spend, give, and save as needed.

CHAPTER 15

Retiring Well

Who doesn't want to retire? Most of us look forward to that day when we can wake up and no longer have to go to work. But is this God's desire for us? It depends. What do you mean by no longer working? Do you mean no longer going to a place of employment to obtain income that is needed to meet your living expenses? That could be God's desire for you, assuming you use your newfound extra time and energy in ways that honor Him. If you mean spending your remaining years living as selfishly as possible, then I think all of us recognize this wouldn't be God's will for any of His people.

This means there are good and bad, right and wrong ways to retire. In this chapter, we will discuss some of the ways we can be good stewards of our retirement years. If we are fortunate enough to be blessed with not having to work anymore, we want to continue working for our Lord.

While God doesn't prohibit retired people (or any people for that matter) from enjoying golf, social functions, or other pleasurable pursuits, these activities shouldn't be the focus of our lives.

What comes to mind when you think of retirement?

Describe how unbelievers are likely to view retirement.

Describe how you think believers should view retirement.

A HISTORY LESSON

Retirement began as an inappropriate response to social issues.

How does the world's view of retirement differ from God's?

Why should the origin of the concept of retirement affect our view of the way retirement is typically handled by the world?

RETIRE INTO CHRISTIAN SERVICE

We might retire from an earthly job,
but we never retire from serving Christ.

Describe three ways retired people can continue serving God.

Retired People Can Mentor

---

*Mentoring and instructing younger people is one of the
primary ministries God has given to older people.*

What value does the older generation offer the younger?

Describe three ways an older saint can encourage a younger believer.

What are three ways an older man can mentor a younger man?

What are three ways an older woman can mentor a younger woman?

Retired People Can Pray

---

*Generations of people have been impacted by
the faithful prayers of elderly people.*

What do you think it means to be "dead even while living"?

Why do you think God would want older people to spend so much time in prayer?

Retired People Can Assist

Why do you think God has requirements for people whose support comes from the church?

Why aren't older people expected to serve with the same vigor as when they were younger?

Slowing Down the Wrong Way

We may lack the energy we had earlier in life, but we should still be as committed to using the energy we still have for His glory.

What are some things older people might not be able to do that they did when they were younger?

Slowing Down the Right Way

If retired people in our day want to help, they should have no trouble finding ways.

What are three practical ways older people can assist younger people?

Considering your strengths and gifts, what are three ways you can help others if God makes it possible for you to retire?

COMBINE FAITH AND WISDOM WHEN PLANNING FOR RETIREMENT

Plan for retirement (wisdom) while trusting God (faith).

What does it mean to combine faith and wisdom?

Provide three examples of what it looks like to combine faith and wisdom.

As you plan for retirement, what does it look like for you to choose the path of faith and wisdom?

Being able to retire is a wonderful blessing, but with blessings come responsibilities and accountability. Yes, we can work toward and look forward to retirement, but we should be committed to using that retirement in ways that please God.

Retire into Christian service. Find spiritually beneficial ways you can invest the remaining time and energy God has given you so that you run the rest of your race well. You can mentor the next generation, pray for those around you, and assist others in small yet helpful ways.

CHAPTER 16

The Greatest Riches

M ay I commend you for all your hard work and making it this far? It has been no small task to read through the book and answer all the questions in the workbook. You have done so much in your pursuit to manage your finances God's way. Yet what if I told you that everything you have learned and worked for up to this point would be meaningless without one thing: a committed relationship with Christ? Ultimately, isn't it for Him that we do everything we do? Don't we want to be good stewards so we can best serve and please Him?

Beautifully, so much of what we have learned only increases our understanding of, and by extension, appreciation of, the gospel of Jesus Christ. Why is that? In the Bible, God explains the gospel using financial terms. Of all the ways God could have chosen to illustrate the gospel, He chose to use financial terms such as *debt, redeem, ransom, pay, impute, poor, rich.*

Understanding these words will help you to better understand what Jesus did for you. My hope is this last chapter will serve to increase your affection for your Lord and Savior.

What are some ways that manna serves as a picture of money?

How does Paul's citation of Exodus 16:18 reinforce the truth of where our resources come from?

MANNA AND MONEY

---

*What Israel was and wasn't supposed to do with manna
resembles what we are and aren't supposed to do with money.*

How might God use money in our lives like He used manna in the lives of the Israelites?

Providing and Testing

How are money and manna both tests of stewardship?

Avoiding Greediness and Wastefulness

---

*The Israelites needed manna like we need money, but they
had to avoid being greedy like we must avoid being greedy.*

How could having too much manna and too much money cause problems?

Learning to Save

How is the balance that must be struck with manna like the balance that must be struck with money?

Enforced Differently

---

*In the church, under the New Covenant, people are cared
for not because it is enforced, but because God burdens His
people to give...willingly, sacrificially, and generously.*

How are those in the church provided for differently than the Israelites were
provided for in the wilderness?

THE TRUE AND GREATER BREAD FROM HEAVEN

---

*If we really want to appreciate the manna, we must
look beyond the physical to the spiritual.*

Why should we seek God daily for our provision?

How is Jesus the true and greater bread from heaven?

THE GOSPEL IS FINANCIAL

---

*[The greatest riches] aren't physical. They
can't be touched, minted, or printed.*

Why do you think God explains the gospel financially?

Debt

———————

We have this debt whether we're rich, poor, young, or old.

———————

What is the worst debt we have?

How can we have this debt forgiven?

Redeem

How is Jesus our Redeemer?

Ransom

———————

The ransom is the payment the redeemer makes to deliver someone from the consequences of their debt.

———————

What ransom is required to redeem a person?

Pay

*Jesus paid the debt when He died on the cross and
took the punishment that our sins deserve.*

What is required for God to remain just?

Impute

What does double imputation refer to?

JESUS'S WORK AND OUR CONDITION

Jesus was anointed to preach the gospel to the poor.

How are we brokenhearted, captive, blind, and oppressed?

What does Jesus do that remedies us of these spiritual conditions?

Spiritually Poor

---

*The reason we (1) must be redeemed, (2) need Christ's
righteousness imputed to our accounts, (3) have debt, and
(4) require a ransom is, simply put, we're poor.*

How are we all poor regardless of how much money we have?

Recognizing Our Spiritual Poverty

---

*The kingdom of heaven belongs to them because
they will put their faith in Christ to receive His
righteousness and have Him pay their debt.*

How can the Bible say that the poor are blessed?

Why are those who think they are spiritually rich in so much danger?

RICH IN CHRIST

---

*If you experience the second birth, you won't experience the second
death: "Blessed and holy is the one who shares in the first resurrection.
Over such the second death has no power" (Revelation 20:6).*

Describe the two births.

Describe the two deaths.

THE PRAYERS FOR YOU

Nobody wants you to be able to manage your finances well more than Jesus Himself.

What does it mean that Jesus is regularly making intercession for us?

How does Jesus satisfy our every need in ways that money cannot?

I hope and pray that *Your Finances God's Way* has been a blessing to you as you've studied how you can better handle one of your greatest stewardships. I'm sure that because you made your way through this workbook, you have identified ways to better manage your money, and most importantly, serve Christ. May you experience a healthier and more joyful relationship with Him for many years to come!

If I can leave you with one precious truth to keep in mind, it is this: If you are a Christian, the gospel is at work in your life to help you obey. Yes, following Christ and managing your finances God's way can be challenging, but remember Paul's words: "I toil, struggling with all his energy that he powerfully works within me" (Colossians 1:29). Yes, you are working hard, but at the same time, God is working powerfully in your life to help you obey Him and experience the fullness of the blessings He has for you.

Appendix

At the link below, you will find budget worksheets that you can use for your financial planning. My hope is that these worksheets will enable you to put into practice the principles you have learned in this book.

https://www.scottlapierre.org/book/your-finances-gods-way/budgets/

Notes

---

1. "American Psychological Association Survey Shows Money Stress Weighing on Americans' Health Nationwide," *American Psychological Association*, https://www.apa.org/news/press/releases/2015/02/money-stress.

2. "Planning and Progress Study," *Northwestern Mutual*, October 11, 2021, https://news.northwesternmutual.com/planning-and-progress-2018.

3. For example:

    Romans 11:25—"I do not desire, brethren, that you should be ignorant of this mystery" (NKJV). Then Paul explained the mystery to them.

    1 Corinthians 12:1—"Concerning spiritual gifts, brethren, I do not want you to be ignorant" (NKJV). Then Paul taught them about spiritual gifts.

    2 Corinthians 1:8—"We do not want you to be ignorant, brethren, of our trouble which came to us in Asia" (NKJV). Then Paul explained their trouble.

    1 Thessalonians 4:13—"I do not want you to be ignorant, brethren, concerning those who have fallen asleep." Then Paul explained what had happened to those who had fallen asleep.

4. S.A. Beeson, "The effect of writing after reading on college nursing students' factual knowledge and synthesis of knowledge," *Journal of Nursing Education*, 35(6), (1996): 258-263.

5. P.A. Mueller and D.M. Oppenheimer, "The pen is mightier than the keyboard: Advantages of longhand over laptop note taking," *Psychological Science*, 25(6), (2014): 1159-1168.

About the Author

Scott is the senior pastor of Woodland Christian Church in Woodland, Washington, and a conference speaker. He holds an MA in biblical studies from Liberty University. Scott and his wife, Katie, grew up together in northern California, and God has blessed them with nine children, with the ninth on the way when the above photograph was taken. You can contact Pastor Scott or learn more about him at the following:

- Website: www.scottlapierre.org
- Facebook: @ScottLaPierreMinistries
- YouTube: @ScottLaPierre
- Twitter: @PastorWCC
- Instagram: @PastorWCC

Subscribe to Pastor Scott's newsletter (www.scottlapierre.org/subscribe) and receive:

- Free gifts and resources such as videos of his conference messages and guest preaching
- Updates on his ministry, including his upcoming books, and invitations to the book launch teams
- Insights into his life and family

Would you like to invite Scott to a speaking event?

Pastor Scott is a frequent speaker at churches, conferences, and retreat centers. He speaks on a variety of topics that build up believers and serve as an outreach to share Christ with your community.

For more information, including sample messages and endorsements, please visit: www.scottlapierre.org/conferences-and-speaking.

If you would like to contact Scott for a speaking engagement, please do so here: www.scottlapierre.org/contact/.

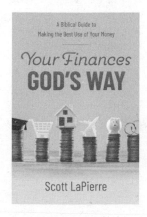

YOUR FINANCES GOD'S WAY

Financial insecurity can be one of the greatest threats to your personal well-being—but the good news is that even when you have less to spend, you can use what God has provided to thrive. In *Your Finances God's Way*, you'll identify negative money management habits you need to break and positive habits that should take their place.

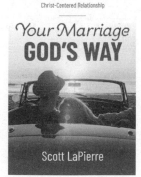

YOUR MARRIAGE GOD'S WAY

With *Your Marriage God's Way*, you'll learn what the Bible reveals about God's original design for the unbreakable commitment between a man and a woman, and how you can have a healthy and joyful relationship centered on Christ.

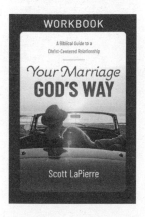

YOUR MARRIAGE GOD'S WAY WORKBOOK

This interactive companion to *Your Marriage God's Way* invites you to work together with your spouse to take a closer look at the biblical principles for a healthy, Christ-centered marriage relationship and make them an active part of your own union.

To learn more about Harvest House books and
to read sample chapters, visit our website:

www.HarvestHousePublishers.com

HARVEST HOUSE PUBLISHERS
EUGENE, OREGON